The Pioneers of Contemporary China
中国时代先锋人物

黄旭华

Huang Xuhua

江　雪　编著
吴　洲　翻译

Sinolingua
华语教学出版社

First Edition 2021
Fourth Printing 2024

ISBN 978-7-5138-2103-2
Copyright 2021 by Sinolingua Co., Ltd
Published by Sinolingua Co., Ltd
24 Baiwanzhuang Street, Beijing 100037, China
Tel: (86) 10-68320585 68997826
Fax: (86) 10-68997826 68326333
http://www.sinolingua.com.cn
E-mail: hyjx@sinolingua.com.cn
Printed by Beijing Hucais Culture Communication Co., Ltd

Printed in the People's Republic of China

Contents

第一章 "弃医从船"的选择 ················ 3

第二章 "土办法"里出潜艇 ············ 19

第三章 碧波深处敢破浪 ················ 29

第四章 回首一生不为名 ················ 39

Chapter One　Choosing Shipbuilding Instead of Medicine ················ 51

Chapter Two　Building a Nuclear Submarine from Scratch ················ 65

Chapter Three　Diving Deep into the Ocean ·· 73

Chapter Four　Living a Life Not for Fame ······· 81

2019年9月29日，人民大会堂内庄严肃穆、华灯璀璨。习近平主席庄重地将共和国勋章颁发给一位老人。老人头发雪白，慈眉善目，肩背笔直，步伐矫健，浑身都透出一股昂扬的精神。共和国勋章是中华人民共和国最高荣誉勋章，专门授予在保卫和建设国家过程中做出巨大贡献、建立卓越功勋的杰出人士。截至2020年8月，全中国获得这项荣誉的只有9个人。

　　那么，这位慈祥的老人家是谁？他为何能获得中国的最高荣誉？

　　这位看上去和邻家爷爷一般慈祥的老人名叫黄旭华，被称为"中国核潜艇之父"。

他毕生都奋斗在中国核潜艇事业的开拓和发展中，带领团队成功研制了中国第一代核潜艇，为中国的海基核力量（建立在以海军的水面舰艇或潜艇作为核武器发射平台的核力量）实现从无到有的历史性跨越做出了卓越的贡献。

这样一位功勋卓著的老人家，在记者采访他的时候，还是那样平静而谦和。他带着微笑回忆了自己的一生，在谈话的结尾，他有点儿羞涩又骄傲地说了一句话："黄旭华，你这一生还是了不起的。"大家都被老人的风趣幽默逗乐了。

黄旭华这了不起的人生，要从他少年时期的选择说起……

第一章
"弃医从船"的选择

1924年2月,黄旭华出生在广东海丰的一个乡村医生家庭。那一年,对中国乃至整个世界来说都是不平凡的。时代风云变化,伟大的革命家列宁在这一年去世,而人类科技的进步成功实现了人工诱发核反应。在中国,与核科技紧密相关的两个人——黄旭华和邓稼先,先后呱呱坠地。他们将支撑起中国核科技事业辉煌的发展。但那时,黄旭华的父母抱着这个新生儿的时候,并不曾预想过这个孩子会和国家、和时代有多么强的联系,只盼望他自立自强,于是按照家中的族谱为他取名——黄绍强。

黄旭华的父母曾在福音医院做过医生，后来创办了"育黎药房"，治病救人，乐善好施，在当地赢得了很好的名声。在这样的家庭中成长起来的黄旭华深受父母影响，他爱学习，关心社会和普通百姓的生活。从很小的时候开始，他就决心继承父母的事业，做一名救死扶伤的医生。

如果一直保持童年的梦想，在一个和平的年代里，黄旭华也许能做一个很好的医生。可是，在那样动荡的年代里，许多人的的命运发生了转变。黄旭华就是那个时代典型的中国人——把自身的事业和国家的命运联系在一起，终生不悔。而这个改变，要从黄旭华14岁时说起。14岁那年，黄旭华该上中学了。那正是1938年，日本侵略者疯狂入侵中国，强占中国的土地，屠杀无辜平民，制造了惨绝人寰的南京大屠杀。时代的

动荡让学校难以放下一张安静的书桌。对14岁的黄旭华来说，因为日寇入侵，家附近已经没有学校可以供他入学读书了。不愿放弃求学的黄旭华决定和大哥一起去寻找迁走的聿怀中学。聿怀中学建于1877年，是广东地区历史最悠久、学风最淳厚的中学之一。1937年，抗日战争爆发的时候，时任聿怀中学校长的陈泽霖先生带领师生迁徙到揭西山区。在艰苦卓绝的物质环境下，陈校长仍然坚持办学。悠久的历史、良好的学风和校长的风骨吸引了不少学子和家长。黄旭华和大哥也是其中之一。他第一次辞别父母，背着包袱，和大哥踏上追随聿怀中学的山路。

　　一路上，他们既要躲避日寇的轰炸，又要忍受漫长路途的艰辛。他们爬过一座座山，蹚过一条条河。他们不停地走啊走，走了整整四天，终于在揭西的山区里找到了聿怀中学，成功入学。在这所用稻草搭起来的简陋学校里，老师们随身带着小黑板，在敌机的轰鸣声中给同学们上课。警报一来，老师们利索地提起小黑板，同学们熟练地抓起书本，一起躲进树林；警报消除后他们再出来继续上课。可即使是在这样艰苦的条件下，黄旭华依旧没有得到长时间的安稳读书时光。日寇的轰炸越来越密集，炮火声越来越频繁。为了师生的生命安全，学校只能宣布解散。无学可上的黄旭华只能继续去寻找学校。去哪里呢？哪里才没有日寇的战火呢？黄旭华也不知道。

年少的黄旭华在炮火声中向前，一路走一路找，越走越远，从广东的梅县、韶关一直走到了广西的桂林。1941年的桂林还没被日军强占，还能容纳学子们求学。进入桂林中学读书的黄旭华决定将自己的名字从黄绍强改为"黄旭华",取自"旭日荣华"之意。"旭日荣华"这四个字表现了他的愿望——希望我们的民族能够像太阳一样升起,永远充满光和热;像花朵开放一样,生机勃勃,幸福美丽。只有国家富强美丽了,人民才能不再遭受苦难。

　　好景不长,覆巢之下岂有完卵?1944年,日寇的战火又开始吞噬桂林。再度失学的黄旭华想不明白:为什么日本人可以那么疯狂地轰炸我们的城市?为什么日本人可以那么无情地屠杀我们的人民?为什么我们中国人想要好好生活、好好读书却总是背井离乡、到处流浪?带着疑惑、痛苦,20岁的黄旭华和许多同胞一起踏上了流浪迁徙的路途。两个月,一千公里,九死一生的黄旭华终于到了重庆,进入到国民政府为流亡学生开办的大学特设先修班学习。

一路奔波磨难，一路哀鸿遍野，让黄旭华意识到，如果国家积贫积弱就会被别人欺负，老百姓就无法获得安定的生活。那么，要想国家富强、人民安定，渺小的个人该怎么做？年轻的黄旭华认为：要去制造飞机捍卫国家的领空，驱赶日本人的战斗机；要去制造军舰抵御外敌的炮火，打击日本人的嚣张气焰。怀着这样朴素的愿望，流浪中的黄旭华决定放弃医学，选择航空或者造船，将自己的一生奉献给祖国。和孙中山、鲁迅一样，自小立志从医的黄旭华将自己的志愿和国家的命运联系在了一起，投身到国家更需要的行业。这一次人生志愿的改变，不是为了追求个人的荣华富贵，而是为了报效祖国。

　　1945年，黄旭华既获得了当时的中央大学航空系的保送，又收到了国立交通大学造船系的录取通知。自小生长在海边的黄旭华决定去上海，进入造船系，去制造军舰，做祖国海上的守卫者。

　　国立交通大学的造船系是当时中国的第一个造船系，拥有一大批从英美学成归来、立志报效祖国的船舶学家。黄旭华在这里不仅学习了许多扎实、先进的船舶技术，更是在精神上直接受到老师们爱国、敬业精神的感染，受用一生。他的老师辛一心曾是留学英国的俊才，是当代中国船舶设计和科学研究机构的创始人。在中国处于风雨飘摇之际，辛一心毅然回国，用自己在英国学到的造船技术报效国家。他一面做船舶实业救国，一面在大学里教书育人，传授船舶技术。他讲课的时候，一方面要求学生在学习每一门课时牢记造船的三个基本需求——"不能沉、不能翻、开得动"，另一方面则以实际的爱国行动感染着每一个求学的学子。他的专业理念和爱国精神影响了黄旭华和同学们的一生。几十年后，黄旭华参与研制核潜艇时依旧牢记着老师的话。

在大学里，黄旭华对国家、社会的认识更加深刻。抗日战争胜利后，黄旭华发现，虽然老百姓不再遭受日寇炮火的摧残，暂时能够安定下来生产、生活，但是，辛苦劳作的普通老百姓仍然吃不饱、穿不暖，而国民党的高官及其亲属却生活奢华。不久，黄旭华就参加了进步社团——山茶社，积极参与进步活动。那时，黄旭华和山茶社的社员们常聚在一起唱歌。他们最喜欢唱的歌是："山那边哟好地方，一片稻田黄又黄。你要吃饭得做工哟，没人给你放牛羊。"是呀，工作得靠自己，幸福的生活也要靠自己争取。可在国民党的腐败统治下，老百姓累死累活，哪里有幸福的地方呢!

现实生活中,黄旭华帮助过进步同学逃脱追捕,积极参加进步活动,表演进步话剧……在大学里,积极又活跃的黄旭华受到了中国共产党地下组织的关注。1946年,一位地下党员找到黄旭华,问:"你对共产党有什么看法?"黄旭华的第一个念头就是,共产党能带领着大家找到"山那边的好地方"。他当即表示,共产党在哪里,哪里就是好地方。很快,黄旭华和一些进步的同学就一起参加了交通大学的"护校运动"。

1946年,为了继续打内战,国民政府压缩交通大学的教育经费,命令交通大学停办航运系和轮机系,并要交通大学改名为"国立南洋工学院"。交通大学不仅面临师生衣食不足的困境,还可能保不住校名。当时的校长吴保丰和学生代表到南京请愿,却遭到国民政府官员的训斥，他们不愿意聆听交通大学师生的心声。这激起了交通大学全体师生的愤怒。1947年5月13日，3000多交通大学的学生冲破阻拦，去上海火车站北站，打算坐火车去南京请愿，这其中就有黄旭华。当时国民政府为了阻拦学生，下命令把火车站里的火车都开走，把火车司机和铁道工人都调走。交通大学的同学们一边派人去找铁道工人，一边靠着自己在学校学习的铁路和火车专业知识，自己开起了火车。"轰隆隆，轰隆隆"……这辆车头上写着"交大万岁"的火车被开了起来。黄旭华就组织其余的同学一起唱《国际歌》《马赛曲》。在歌声中，在火车声中，黄旭华和同学们以实际行动捍卫了交通大学的尊严。护校运动取得了成功！

　　1949年，黄旭华成为一名中国共产党

党员，大学毕业后正式进入了解放后的上海船舶建造处工作。他决心将自己的一生奉献给他所选择的、所热爱的事业，和祖国一起成长。

此后，黄旭华加入中国核潜艇研制工作，和同事们一起从无到有设计、研发中国自己的核潜艇。1970年12月26日，中国第一艘核潜艇下水。1974年8月1日，中国第一艘核潜艇加入海军战斗序列。历经12年，在不依靠任何外国技术和人员帮助的情况下，中国完全凭借自己的努力研制出了核潜艇，距离世界上第一艘核潜艇下水仅16年的时间。黄旭华兴奋地说："这完完全全是我们中国自己的核潜艇！"当年那个弃医从船的20岁青年已经50岁了，从一个风华正茂的年轻人变成了一位成熟稳重的中年人。时光在变，容颜在改变，唯一不变的是黄旭华将人生的事业和祖国的发展紧密联系在一起的爱国报国之心。

第二章
"土办法"里出潜艇

黄旭华和研究团队是依靠什么造出了世界最核心、最机密技术的核潜艇呢？这还得从中国核潜艇的研制说起。

1958年，黄旭华已经和爱人结婚，并有了可爱的大女儿，生活美满幸福。有一天，他接到领导的通知，让他去北京出差。黄旭华来不及准备什么就去了北京，这一去就留在了那里。原来，当时国际形势风云变幻，美国对中国实施封锁政策，中苏两国关系迅速恶化。面对世界两大巨头的威胁，中国共产党决定自力更生，通过经济、军事国防等多方面的发展来增强综合国力。于是，研制

核潜艇便被提上了日程。黄旭华曾经参加过苏联援助中国的舰船转让制造和仿制工作，自身的专业技术过硬，因此被选调为此次核潜艇研制的工作人员。

对于当时的中国来说，这是绝密的工作，也是非常艰苦的工作。苏联撤回了所有的援助专家，国内缺乏研制核潜艇的专业人员。当时选派的29名工作骨干平均年龄不到30岁，连核潜艇是什么样都没见过。"一穷二白""一无所知"，这两个成语大概是能最恰当地形容中国建设核潜艇初期情况的词语。

没有技术，我们自己琢磨！没有经验，我们自己摸索！黄旭华和同事们依靠最朴实的土办法去制造潜艇，攻坚克难，不断创新，最终成功研制出了中国自己的核潜艇。而他们用的土办法，现在说给大家听，也许大家都会觉得不可思议。

在20世纪50年代末，中国缺少基本的核潜艇研制条件。尽管当时美国和苏联的核潜艇先后下水，但相关的信息都是高度保密的。对于当时中国的研究人员来说，遇到的最大困难就是他们根本不知道核潜艇长什么样，他们要做的事情听来有点儿像天方夜谭。不过，当时中国的哪项事业不是从一穷二白干起来的呢？中国人从不缺少拼劲儿和钻研劲儿。怎么办？黄旭华和他的同事们一方面尽可能去搜罗国际报刊中有关核潜艇的零星信息，进行信息拼凑，另一方面则开始研究玩具模型。

玩具模型？这和核潜艇有什么关系？原来，当时正好有个工作人员从美国带回来两个核潜艇儿童玩具模型。黄旭华他们琢磨着，这玩具的造型结构应该和真实的核潜艇有类似之处吧！于是，他们就把这两个玩具拆了装，装了拆，不断琢磨相关的零件设备。依靠着零散的资料、玩具模型和他们的创新想象，黄旭华和同事们就这样一点点琢磨出了核潜艇的构造和样式。当时谁也不知道凭着这点儿东西能不能研制出来，但大家都在不断地互相打气。黄旭华后来回忆从玩具模型开始造核潜艇时仍然很兴奋，他带着点儿天真气地说："我当时就想，核潜艇也没什么大不了的嘛！再尖端的东西，都是在常规技术的基础上综合创新出来的，并不神秘。"就是靠着这股子"没什么大不了"的拼劲儿和综合创新，他们突破了研制核潜艇的第一大难关。

紧接着，他们面临着核潜艇研制技术中的第二大难关——数据计算。核潜艇研制的技术非常复杂，涉及大量的数据计算，尤其是核潜艇中最关键的核动力装置、水滴线型艇体、艇体结构、人工大气环境、水下通信、惯性导航系统和发射装置七大核心内容。一旦有任何一个数据出了错，研制工作就会功亏一篑。而那时候中国并没有现在这样先进的计算机和计算能力。甚至，当时中国的第一台计算机"103"机才刚诞生，运算速度仅为每秒30次。怎么办？怎么算？

　　黄旭华和他的同事们再一次发挥执着、创新的拼劲儿，依靠传统的算盘、计算尺和磅秤来完成数据的计算。小小的算盘"噼里啪啦"不停地响，却诞生了中国第一艘核潜艇中许多重要的数据。那些计算不是简简单单的加减乘除，而是需要涉及三角函数、对数等各种复杂且高难度的运算公式和模型。但恰恰是这样夜以继日的算盘计算攻克了数据计算的难关。黄旭华至今还保留着一把北京生产的"前进"牌算盘。那是当年他们计

算核潜艇数据时使用的算盘。黄旭华每次看到这把算盘就会想起当年研制核潜艇时攻坚克难的日子，既艰苦但又充满创造的乐趣。

平时称东西的磅秤怎么用来造核潜艇呢？黄旭华和同事们分成两到三组，分别用一台磅秤称一个个的零件。只要结果不同就重新再来，直到得出一模一样的数据为止。工作多年的黄旭华一直牢记着读书时老师教给他们的关于造船的三个基本需求——不能沉、不能翻、开得动。所以，他和同事们都耐着性子细心完成每一次数据计算。施工完成后，为了保证材料的使用没有问题，他连拿出来的管道、电缆、边角余料都要过秤，不肯放过，黄旭华被同事们开玩笑地称为"斤斤计较的设计师"。正是靠着"斤斤计较"的精神，靠着"土里土气"的算盘、磅秤，中国第一艘数千吨的核潜艇下水后试潜、定重测试的数据和设计值完全吻合。

从1958年召集团队到1970年第一艘核潜艇下水，黄旭华和他的同事们没有外国相关专业人员的援助，没有先进的技术支持，全靠着自己的聪明才智步步创新，靠着"土办法"一一计算，制造出中国第一艘核潜艇。这其中饱含着多少汗水，又饱含着多少智慧。黄旭华没有提及当时的艰苦，反倒因为大家能利用这些土办法创造出核潜艇而深感骄傲和自豪。

第三章

碧波深处敢破浪

1970年，中国第一艘核潜艇下水。

1974年，中国第一艘核潜艇交付海军使用。

但直到1988年，中国的第一艘核潜艇才进行了深潜试验，彻底完成了研制的全过程。这是为什么呢？

原来，中国的核潜艇研制一直是在北方进行的。北方海域的水浅，核潜艇问世18年一直没能进行极限深度的深潜试验。这个深潜试验也从技术、心理两个方面考验着黄旭华和同事们。

首先，核潜艇的深潜试验是十分危险的。

黄旭华后来接受采访时谈到："艇上一块扑克牌大小的钢板，潜入水下数百米后，承受的水的压力是1吨多。100多米长的艇体，任何一块钢板不合格、一条焊缝有问题、一个阀门封闭不足，都可能导致艇毁人亡。"也就是说，核潜艇在深潜时，只要出任何一点儿问题都可能导致重大的失败和惨剧发生。我们用"土办法"造出来的核潜艇能行吗？

其次，核潜艇的深潜试验不是没有牺牲的先例。1963年4月10日，美国当时先进的核潜艇"长尾鲨"号在波士顿东部大海进行深潜试验，结果，深潜失败，核潜艇变成了一堆碎片，艇上129人无一生还。后来美国进行调查，发现可能是"长尾鲨"号的一根海水管道破裂，导致海水大量涌入舱内浸泡了电线进而影响了电气系统，使得核潜艇沉入海底。虽然这个事件距离中国核潜艇深潜试验已经20多年了，但是这惨烈的结局如同阴云笼罩在黄旭华和同事们的头上。大家都有一个疑问：我们的核潜艇全是自己靠着土办法做出来的，一旦下潜到极限深度，会不会像"长尾鲨"号一样一去不返？

当时，虽然试潜相关人员已经做好牺牲的思想准备，有的甚至写好了遗书，但是沉重的思想负担仍然影响了整支团队的士气。谁不珍惜自己的生命呢？谁不害怕未知的危险呢？牺牲的决心和怀疑、恐惧的心理同时笼罩着大家。为此，核潜艇的艇长和政委找到了已经是总设计师的黄旭华，想让他给大家打打气，振作士气。黄旭华沉思了一晚，第二天就带着技术骨干直接来到了深潜试验团队的会议室，果断宣布："这样吧，我跟你们一起下去！"这句话就像一滴水掉进了油锅，会议室里一下子就沸腾起来。在核潜艇

的研制历史上，从来没有总设计师直接参与深潜试验过程的先例。而且这时的黄旭华已经64岁，不再是年轻小伙子了，多年的苦干让他的身体也没那么强壮。大家都认为黄旭华冒这个险没有意义，坚决不同意黄旭华跟着下海。面对大家的反对，黄旭华语重心长地说："第一，我们这次去，不是去'光荣'，而是要去把数据拿回来；第二，所有的设计都留了足够安全的系数；第三，我们复查了三个月，很有信心。"正是黄旭华的"拿数据""有信心"安抚了整个试潜团队的军心，让大家变得乐观起来，不再只想到深潜的危险和恐惧。

其实，黄旭华心里也紧绷绷的。核潜艇研制到了这一步，必须成功！但是，如果，如果真的失败了……那后果黄旭华也不敢想象。可他还是决定下海，就像年少时决定顶着日寇的炮火去寻找学校一样，就像当年放弃幼时学医的梦想选择造船一样。这时候，妻子李世英成为他最坚定的支持者。李世英也从事核潜艇研制工作，他们志同道合。当得知黄旭华要下海时，她抛开了担忧和顾虑，以一种坚定的姿态站在了黄旭华的身后。她知道，这时候黄旭华需要的是毫无保留的支持。尽管知晓危险性，但李世英坚定地说："你是总设计师，必须下去，不然队伍都带不好，没人听你的话。再说，你要为艇上人的生命负责到底。"妻子的支持让黄旭华更加坚定了参加下潜试验的决心。他身先士卒的精神和对核潜艇的信心感染了试验团队，稳定了军心，保证了试验的顺利进行。

　　终于到了深潜试验的这一天——1988年4月29日。那一天，南海的浪有点儿大，浪头达到了1米多，但天气很不错。大家准备就绪后，潜艇开始慢慢下潜。10米，10米，10米……5米，5米，5米……1米，1米，1米……潜艇下潜的状态从最初的10米一停到后来的1米一停。而随着下潜深度的加大，钢板承受的水压也越来越大，"咔嗒咔嗒"的声响也越来越大。试验团队每一个人的心都被揪得紧紧的。团队中除了操作的声音、"咔嗒咔嗒"的艇舱声，就只剩下紧张的呼吸声了。黄旭华全神贯注地记录和测量着各种数据，仿佛什么都没有听见。终于，核潜艇到达了极限深度——300米。没有问题！潜艇岿然不动，完好无损。接下来，潜艇还要顶着巨大的水压上升到海面。怀着激动、忐忑的心情，大家静静地等候着。上升，上升，上升……距离海面280米，200米，150米，100米！直到上升到安全深度，大家一下子就沸腾起来。他们抱着彼此大笑，拍着

彼此的肩膀流泪。连一向从容镇定的黄旭华也和大家一样兴奋得难以自持——我们终于成功了！在场的每个人都知道，这成功来得有多么不容易！

在深潜试验的基础上，1988年下半年，中国完成了水下发射导弹的试验。这意味着中国真正具备了水下核反击能力，真正通过自身发展具备了保卫国家的能力。为着祖国的核潜艇事业，为着中国的复兴发展，黄旭华执着于造船事业，乐在其中。他曾害怕或是怀疑过吗？也许是有的。但是每当重要关头，他都不会退缩。黄旭华以坚定的姿态带领团队披荆斩棘，乘风破浪。黄旭华的一生，可以用《钢铁是怎样炼成的》里保尔的话来描述：

"生命属于每一个人只有一次。人的一生应当这样度过——当他回首往事时，不因虚度年华而悔恨，也不因碌碌无为而愧疚。这样，在临死的时候，他就能够说：我把自己的整个生命和全部精力都献给了世界上最壮丽的事业——为人类解放而奋斗。"

第四章
回首一生不为名

"黄旭华,你这一生还是了不起的。"

黄旭华笑着、欣慰地评价自己的一生,满足地说自己"了不起",但却从不将功劳独揽在自己身上。在中国,大家都称黄旭华为"中国核潜艇之父"。但他并不接受,他说自己"仅仅是核潜艇研究战线中的一个成员"。

不揽名,不慕利,乐观积极,正是黄旭华这一生的写照。

1958年,黄旭华刚开始参与绝密的核潜艇研究工作时就知道这是一份艰苦而且默默无闻的工作。他的工作内容连自己最亲密的

家人都不能告知。黄旭华毫不犹豫地接过祖国交予的重任，加入研制团队，几十年如一日默默地在工作岗位上奉献，甘心做核潜艇设计研制事业中的无名英雄。在这个过程中，家人对他的支持就像厚实的土地对大树的支撑一样，起着非常重要的作用。

　　黄旭华的妻子李世英也是一位科研人员。她的性格沉稳果敢，与丈夫的感情也非常好。黄旭华当年去北京长时间没有回来时，李世英就隐约猜测到自己的丈夫可能会从事什么样的重要工作了。她没有刨根问底，也没有抱怨，只是用实际行动支持着丈夫的工作。家里的各种家务、养育孩子的艰辛，她都一个人承受下来。后来，李世英又一个人带着孩子从上海千里迢迢搬家到北京，再从北京搬到黄旭华工作的海岛。住在海岛上的那些年，一到冬天储存煤球的时候，李世英就要带着孩子一起，花很大的力气把几百斤煤球运回家。在这样独自支撑家庭的岁月里，李世英还能幽默地打趣黄旭华。每次黄旭华休假回家时，李世英远远看见他就笑着说："客人回家了！"黄旭华也老老实实地称自己为"客人"。他没有为这个家做过什么贡献，常常来也匆匆，去也匆匆，在家里待不到一天就回研究所了。多少年以后，当黄旭华回忆起这些经历时，他对家人所怀有的是深深的歉意和谢意。

　　为黄旭华付出的还有他年迈的父母——因为工作的特殊性质，黄旭华一直不能告诉自己的父母他在做什么。直到1987年，黄旭华的老母亲才知道原来自己的儿子从事的是祖国的核潜艇事业。为此，老人还专门给家里人开了个家庭会议，告诉他们要理解黄旭华，要为他感到骄傲。

中国核潜艇事业能够获得迅猛的发展，离不开千千万万像黄旭华一样的科研人员的奉献，以及他们家人的支持！核潜艇研制成功后，黄旭华在每一次的采访中都率直坦诚地说："我很爱我的妻子、母亲和女儿，我很爱她们。"作为一个从20世纪20年代走来的老人，他如此热情坦诚地说爱，是因为对家人的亏欠，更是因为对家人怀有深沉的感情。他爱着亲人，更爱着国家。为了国家的发展，他永远不后悔自己当年所做的选择。

核潜艇研制工作并不像外人想象的那样报酬丰厚。除了研制核潜艇的技术挑战外，黄旭华和同事们还要面临物质的短缺和生活的艰苦。但这些困难都被黄旭华以吃苦耐劳和乐观的精神——战胜了。

核潜艇研制工作是需要随着进程不断转移地点的。有很长一段时间，黄旭华和同事们都待在荒芜的海岛上。那是渤海湾的葫芦岛——一个离海很近也非常寒冷的地方。常年待在南方的黄旭华第一次踏上葫芦岛的时候，岛上的大风就"将"了他一军。凛冽的大风从四面刮过来，仿佛要把地皮都刮走，到处风沙弥漫。风刮过来的时候，成年人都会站不住脚跟，得抱着树干才稳得下来，大家甚至戏称这风为"抱树风"。环境已经这样恶劣了，生活条件能好点儿吗？事实并非如此。在岛上生活，人们常常见不到一点儿荤腥，让这些平均年龄不到30岁的年轻人馋得发慌。

"今天早上吃什么？"

"白菜炖白菜！"

"中午吃什么？"

"土豆炖白菜！"

"晚上吃什么？"

"土豆炖土豆！"

……

这样的对话几乎天天在研究团队中出现。那时候，最让黄旭华和同事们开心的就是吃"红方"了。"红方"一送来，大家那一天都是笑着的——

"今天吃什么？"

"红方！"

"红方！居然有红方！那我今天要吃两碗高粱饭！"

"你不是平时只吃得下一碗嘛！别逞强。留着，让我帮你吃一碗。"

"那不行，有红方，几碗都吃得下！"

……

他们如此珍视的"红方"是什么呢？说来大家可能不信，"红方"就是豆腐乳。对于天天吃土豆白菜的黄旭华他们来说，一顿

有味道的豆腐乳配上高粱米饭，简直是人间美味。今天，黄旭华回忆起那个艰苦的年代，不仅不觉得辛苦，反而觉得充满了乐趣。这恰恰表现了中国人传统精神中"一箪食，一瓢饮"的文化血脉。

也许正是因为热爱，黄旭华才能如此毫无保留地投入到核潜艇研制的事业中，才能在艰苦的研究工作中取得伟大的成就。而这热爱的背后，是黄旭华不慕名利、吃苦耐劳、乐观昂扬、为国不悔的一生。

今天，黄旭华依旧践行着自己这一生的誓言。90多岁高龄的他乍一看去就像邻家慈祥的老爷爷。他虽然已经不再直接从事核潜艇的研制工作，但每天早上8点半，黄旭华仍然准时走进办公室。他要整理几十年核潜艇研制工作中留下来的资料，把这些资料留给年轻一代人。有时候，黄旭华还会对年轻的核潜艇研究人员进行指导，给他们加油鼓劲。人生已经走到后半程，他依旧没有放弃工作。利用余光，继续发热，直到生命的最后一刻。这是黄旭华最真实的想法。

词作家闫肃2014年写给黄旭华的歌词，也许是对他这一生的最好描述——

"试问大海碧波，何谓以身许国？青丝化作白发，依旧铁马冰河。磊落平生无限爱，尽付无言高歌。"

On September 29, 2019, in the solemn and brightly illuminated Great Hall of the People, President Xi Jinping conferred the Medal of the Republic on an amiable old man with snowy hair and a straight back. Though he was 95 years old, he stepped forward with vibrant, firm steps. The Medal of the Republic is China's highest honor awarded to those outstanding figures who have made tremendous contributions to defending and building the country. As of August 2020, only nine people had received this honor.

Who is this old man? What did he do to deserve China's highest honor?

This man, who looks like a friendly grandpa living

next door, is Huang Xuhua. Known as the "father of China's nuclear submarines," he dedicated his life to the research and development of China's nuclear submarine. He led his team in designing China's first-generation nuclear submarine which marked a historic breakthrough in China's sea-based nuclear forces that are launched from maritime platforms, such as surface ships or submarines.

Despite having such an outstanding record of remarkable meritorious service, he was calm and modest during interview. With a smile, he told the reporter about his life. At the end of the interview, he said shyly but proudly, "Huang Xuhua! Your life has been remarkable after all." Everyone was amused by his humor.

This is the story of the remarkable life of Huang Xuhua, and how it sprung from a choice he made during childhood.

Chapter One

Choosing Shipbuilding Instead of Medicine

In February 1924, Huang Xuhua was born into a village doctor's family in Haifeng, Guangdong Province. That year proved to be eventful and extraordinary for China and the world. It was an age of rapid change. That year, the socialist revolutionary Vladimir Ilyich Lenin passed away, and artificially-induced nuclear reaction was made a reality with scientific and technological advances. Huang Xuhua and another famous Chinese scientist Deng Jiaxian were both born that year, and they would later play a pivotal role in developing the country's nuclear science and technology. Of course, when Huang Xuhua was born, his parents could never imagine how significant a role he would play in China and the world. They simply hoped that he would grow up to be self-reliant and motivated, so they named him Huang Shaoqiang.

His parents used to be doctors at the Gospel Hospital in Haifeng, but later founded their own clinic, the Yuli Pharmacy (*yuli* literally meaning "caring for the ordinary people"). The couple's medical service and philanthropy earned them great respect and popularity among the local people. Under their influence, Huang Xuhua became an avid learner who paid great attention to social issues and the well-being of people. In his childhood, he was determined to become a doctor to heal the sick and save the dying, just as his parents did.

If Huang Xuhua had kept his childhood dream during a time of peace, he might have become a good doctor. But this was not to be. Many people saw their lives upturned during those turbulent years, and he was one of the typical Chinese of that era — those who chose to associate their destiny with that of the country.

His change began when he was 14 years old — an age when he should have been attending middle school. But in 1938, Japanese aggressors ruthlessly invaded China, seized Chinese land and began mercilessly killing innocent Chinese civilians. Among the atrocities was the Nanjing Massacre, a holocaust of unparalleled savagery. The chaotic times made it nearly impossible for schools to hold normal classes. But giving up learning was the last thing on the boy's mind. He decided to follow his eldest brother to look for the relocated Yuhuai High School. Founded in 1877, the school was one of the oldest middle schools in Guangdong and was known for its good academic atmosphere. In 1937 during the War of Resistance Against Japanese Aggression, the headmaster Mr. Chen Zelin led the faculty and students to the mountainous region of Jiexi where they braved all kinds of hardships to keep the school running. The school's history, academic atmosphere, and the headmaster's character appealed to many students and parents, including Huang Xuhua and his eldest brother. They packed up and embarked on the mountain road, setting out for Yuhuai High School. This was the first time that he had ever left his parents.

It was a long, hard journey. They had to avoid air bombings by the Japanese invaders all the way, while climbing mountains and wading across rivers. They kept walking for four days until they found the school. It was a makeshift campus made up of a few thatched cottages, where the teachers each carried a small blackboard and lectured amidst the roar of enemy planes overhead. Whenever the air-raid siren sounded, the teachers would pick up their blackboards and lead the students to hide in the woods. After the alarm ceased, they would come back to resume class. However, Huang Xuhua's time to study in relative peace under such difficult conditions was cut short. The bombings by the Japanese became more intense, and the artillery fire became more frequent, forcing the school to shut down for the safety of the teachers and students. Now Huang Xuhua, a dropout, had to again look for a school where he could study. Where could he go? Was there any place away from the flames of war? He didn't know.

He moved on, braving artillery fire in his search for another school. He went farther and farther, all the way to Guilin in Guangxi. It was 1941, and the Japanese had not occupied Guilin, so finally Huang Xuhua found a place where he could receive an education. He enrolled in Guilin High School where he decided to change his name from Huang Shaoqiang to Huang Xuhua. The new name expressed his wish for the nation to rise up like the early morning sun (旭 *xu*) that radiates light and becomes as vibrant and beautiful as a blossom (华 *hua*). It meant that only when the nation became prosperous, strong and beautiful would the Chinese people no longer suffer.

But, sadly again, the good times did not last long. In 1944, the flames of war had spread to Guilin. Again, Huang Xuhua was forced to drop out of school. He wondered how the Japanese invaders could so wantonly bombard China's cities and ruthlessly kill its people. All Chinese people wanted was to live their lives and study in peace. Why is it all we do is leave our homes and wander around, he wondered. With doubts and pain, Huang Xuhua, now a 20-year-old young man, joined many other compatriots on a long journey westward. For two months they traveled some 1,000 kilometers and endured many hardships, and finally arrived in Chongqing where he enrolled in a special preparatory program offered by the National Government for exiled students.

The hard journey and the plight of his fellow countrymen made Huang Xuhua realize that an impoverished and weak country would only be bullied and end up at the mercy of other countries, leaving its people to struggle. So what could an individual do to make his country prosperous and strong and bring peace to its people? His first thought was to make airplanes to defend China's airspace against the Japanese invaders, and make warships in order to resist enemy gunfire. Huang Xuhua, who had wandered about for years, had decided on these careers as his life path instead of medicine, as he saw that it was the best way to dedicate himself to his motherland. Though he'd been determined to become a doctor just like Dr. Sun Yat-sen and Lu Xun, he saw that it was more important to choose a profession that was more urgently needed by the country. He felt that this was not a time to follow ambition and seek personal prosperity, but rather a time to change the course of his life and serve the motherland, instead.

In 1945, Huang Xuhua was recommended for admission to the Aviation Department of National Central University, but at the same time received a notice of admission to the Shipbuilding Department of the National Chiao Tung University. Since he had lived on the seaside, he opted for the latter, and was determined to build warships to defend China's territorial waters.

The Shipbuilding Department of the National Chiao Tung University was the first of its kind in China. Its teachers included many shipbuilding experts who had studied in the UK and US and had returned to China to serve their country. From them, he learned advanced shipbuilding techniques and also patriotism and professionalism, which exerted a strong influence on him in his entire life. One example was his teacher, Mr. Xin Yixin. He'd been an outstanding student who had studied in the UK, and was the founder of China's ship design and research institutes. Although China was in a state of war, he returned and worked for the country with the knowledge he'd learned in the UK, building up China's shipbuilding industry and imparting shipbuilding technologies at university. In his classes, he demanded that students bear in mind the three basic shipbuilding requirements: "the ship must not sink, not capsize, and it must be able to move." His professionalism and patriotism had a lasting effect on Huang Xuhua and his classmates. He would remember his teacher's words later while getting involved in the research and development of nuclear submarines decades later.

At university, Huang Xuhua acquired a deeper understanding of the state and society. After China achieved victory in the War of Resistance Against Japanese Aggression, its people no longer suffered from Japanese bombings and were able to live and work in peace for the moment. He found, however, that ordinary people still did not have enough food and clothing despite their hard work, but the high-ranking officials of the Kuomintang (the Nationalist Party of China) and their relatives led an extravagant life. It wasn't long afterwards that he joined the

Camellia Society, a progressive social organization, and they would often get together to sing songs. One of their favorite songs went like this:

Oh, there's a good place over the mountain

Where lies a vast expanse of golden rice fields.

To feed yourself, you have to work.

No one else will herd your cattle and sheep.

The meaning of the song was that everyone must work to enjoy a happy life. But under the corrupt rule of the Kuomintang the common people were struggling to survive. Therefore, how could there be happiness?

Huang Xuhua helped progressive classmates escape capture by the Kuomintang, took an active part in progressive activities, and played roles in progressive dramas. His enthusiasm drew the close attention of the underground CPC (Communist Party of China) organization. In 1946, an underground CPC member approached him and asked what he thought of the CPC. The first thought to flash across his mind was that the CPC could lead the people in finding a "good place over the mountain". He immediately replied that wherever the CPC is, it must be a good place. Before long, he and some progressive classmates participated in the student movement to protect the National Chiao Tung University.

In 1946, in order to continue fighting the civil war, the National Government cut spending for the National Chiao Tung University, decreed the suspension of the two departments of shipping and marine engineering, and renamed it the National Nanyang Institute of Engineering. The National Chiao Tung University was unable to provide adequate food and clothing to its teachers and students and was unlikely to retain its original name. University president Wu Baofeng and a few student representatives went to Nanjing to petition against the decree. They were reprimanded by government officials, who even did not bother to hear them out. This infuriated all the teachers and students of the university. On May 13, 1947, over 3,000 students, including Huang Xuhua, broke through the blockades and arrived at the Shanghai North Railway Station, from where they planned to take a train to Nanjing to petition. To stop students from doing this, the government ordered that all the trains leave the station, along with all the drivers and railway workers. The students managed to find one train, however, and operated it themselves, making use of their own railway and train knowledge. A slogan was pasted on the locomotive, reading "Long Live the National Chiao Tung University!" On the train, Huang Xuhua organized other students to sing "The Internationale" and "La Marseillaise" in chorus. Amid the rumbling of the train, the students defended the university's dignity by their actions. The student movement to protect the university was crowned with a success.

In 1949, Huang Xuhua became a member of the Communist Party of China. Upon graduation from university, he was assigned to work at the Shanghai Shipbuilding Office. He was determined to dedicate his life to the career he had chosen and to forge ahead together with the country he loved.

Decades later, he joined China's nuclear submarine research and development team. To design and make China's own nuclear submarine, they had to start from scratch. On December 26, 1970, China's first nuclear submarine was launched, and on August 1, 1974, it was delivered to the PLA Navy. It took China 12 years to independently develop a nuclear submarine without the help of foreign technologies and personnel. This took place just 16 years after the world's first nuclear submarine was launched.

Huang Xuhua said excitedly, "This submarine is one hundred percent made in China." The 20-year-old young man who had chosen shipbuilding instead of medicine was now 50 years old, and had changed from a promising young man to a mature and steady middle-aged man. With the passage of time, his appearance had changed. But unchanged was his enduring patriotism and dedication that would forever bind his lifelong career with the development of China.

Chapter Two

Building a Nuclear Submarine from Scratch

How did Huang Xuhua and his team build one of the world's most secretive and state-of-the-art nuclear submarines without any outside help? The answer lies in the research and development of China's nuclear submarine program.

In 1958, Huang Xuhua got married, and the couple gave birth to a beautiful baby girl. His family life brimmed with happiness. One day, his superior instructed him to go on a business trip to Beijing, and he went right away. China was putting its nuclear submarine program on the agenda. At that time, the US had imposed a blockade against China, and Sino-Soviet relations were deteriorating rapidly. Faced with threats from both superpowers, the Communist Party of China was determined to increase the nation's economic and military strength. Huang Xuhua had been involved in the transfer, manufacture and imitation of ships provided to China by the Soviet Union. Because of his professional competence and experience in this area, he was selected to join the nuclear submarine research and development team.

This mission was top-secret and very difficult. The Soviet Union withdrew all its experts from China, and there was a shortage of nuclear submarine development professionals. The average age of the 29 personnel selected for the mission was under 30. They had no idea what a nuclear submarine even looked like. "Impoverished and backwards" and "utterly ignorant" were perhaps the phrases that best described China's initial conditions for its nuclear submarine program.

Without the technologies and experience, the

team worked to figure it out on their own. In their research and development, Huang Xuhua and his colleagues had to employ the simplest methods, which were quite incredible.

In the late 1950s, China did not have the basic conditions for nuclear submarine development. Although the US and the Soviet Union had launched their own nuclear submarines, they kept all the relevant information and data top-secret. For the Chinese researchers, the biggest difficulty was that they did not even know what a nuclear submarine looked like. But Chinese people are perseverant and resourceful. Huang Xuhua and his colleagues collected bits of information about nuclear submarines from foreign newspapers and periodicals, and also studied toy models.

So what did toy models have to do with nuclear submarines? At that time, one of his colleagues happened to have returned from the US with two nuclear submarine toy models. The team looked at the models and got inspired. They thought perhaps there could be some similarities between the models and a real nuclear submarine in terms of appearance and structure. They dissembled and reassembled the two models again and again to understand the relevant parts and equipment. Based on such bits of information, Huang Xuhua and his colleagues gradually figured out the structure of a nuclear submarine, though no one was sure whether this could actually help them build one. As he recalled this period, he was still very excited. "At that time, I thought it was something that could be accomplished. Even cutting-edge things must be developed through innovation based on conventional technologies." It was with such perseverance and innovation that he and his colleagues made the first major breakthrough in the nuclear submarine program.

The second challenge they met was computing. Nuclear submarines demand extremely complex technologies and vast quantities of data calculation, particularly for its seven core systems — the nuclear power system, the tear drop-shaped hull, the hull structure, the artificial atmospheric environment, the underwater telecommunication system, the inertial navigation system, and the launcher. A mistake in any calculation would ruin the whole endeavor. At that time, however, China had no advanced computers necessary for these computing tasks. In fact, the first Chinese computer, called "Model 103," had just been made, and was only capable of performing 30 calculations per second. What could they do to meet the computing challenge?

Again, Huang Xuhua and his colleagues had to call upon their perseverance and innovation. Their solution was to use abacuses, slide rules, and platform scales. Amidst the clinking of the abacuses, they worked out a lot of important data for China's first nuclear submarine. It is noteworthy that the calculations were not such basic arithmetic as addition, subtraction, multiplication, and division, but involved complex and difficult formulas and models like trigonometric functions and logarithms. Yet the team tackled the calculations with tools as simple as abacuses. Until now, Huang Xuhua still retains an "Advance" abacus made in Beijing, which is one of the abacuses they used to calculate the data. The sight of this abacus always brings to his mind those old days he spent on the nuclear submarine development, which were difficult but very creative as it forced them to find innovative ways to solve their problems.

So how were platform scales used in their calculations? Huang Xuhua and his colleagues split into two or three groups and weighed each part to be installed, making sure its weight matched the design value. For any inconsistencies, the part in question had to be remade or adjusted until it matched. The three basic requirements for shipbuilding engineering — "the ship must not sink, not capsize, and must move forward," which his teacher had taught him at university, had remained firmly engraved on Huang Xuhua's mind. He and his colleagues patiently performed each and every data calculation with the utmost care. After the construction was completed, he even checked the weight of the piping, cabling and other small materials. For this, his colleagues jokingly dubbed Huang Xuhua "a meticulous designer". Thanks to such a commitment to precision and using the simplest calculation tools, China's first nuclear submarine was made. What is more extraordinary is that the submarine, which weighed several thousand tons, showed data completely consistent with the design values during its dive test and weight-balance test.

From 1958 when the team was first formed until 1970 when the first nuclear submarine was launched, Huang Xuhua and his colleagues had no help from foreign professionals or any advanced technical support. They relied solely on their own ingenuity and innovation, and a step-by-step approach using the simplest calculation tools. Their success can be attributed to their hard work and innovation. Though there were many hardships at that time, Huang said nothing. He instead felt pride and a great sense of accomplishment when remembering the trials they endured.

Chapter Three

Diving Deep into the Ocean

In 1970, China's first nuclear submarine was launched.

In 1974, China's first nuclear submarine was delivered to the PLA Navy.

But it was not until 1988 that China's first nuclear submarine completed the deep dive tests, which consummated the entire research and development program. Why did this occur so late?

It turned out that the submarine had been made in northern China where the sea is shallow, and hence the deep dive test — a test dive to its maximum design depth — could not be made until 18 years later. When the time finally came to conduct the test, Huang Xuhua and his team were faced with both technical and psychological challenges.

First, deep dive tests for nuclear submarines are very dangerous. Huang later told journalists, "When a nuclear submarine dives hundreds of meters deep, a steel plate the size of a playing card bears more than one ton of water pressure. For a boat with a length of over 100 meters, any defect in any steel plate, weld seam, or valve sealing could be catastrophic." In other words, when a nuclear submarine dives deep, any existing problem or inaccurate construction design could doom the vessel. Could the submarine which was built under such poor conditions stand the test?

Second, there had been precedents for deadly accidents during nuclear submarine deep dive tests. On April 10, 1963, one such accident took place when the USS Thresher — the then US's most advanced nuclear submarine — was going through a deep dive test in the waters off the east coast of Boston. The dive failed, and the submarine sunk, killing the entire crew of 129. Later investigations discovered that the accident was most likely caused by the rupture of a seawater pipe, which allowed massive quantities of water into the cabin and then soaked the electric wires, causing the failure of the submarine's electrical system. Though almost 20 years had passed since this accident, the tragedy remained a constant cloud hovering over Huang Xuhua and his colleagues. After all, their first nuclear submarine had been developed with simple "homespun" methods. When it dived to extreme depths, what if it went down never to return like the USS Thresher?

The test crew were mentally prepared for possible failure and death, and some had even written their last letters. The whole team suffered from low morale in the face of uncertainty. Who doesn't value his life? Who was not afraid of the unknown dangers? Doubt and fear, mingled with the determination for self-sacrifice, hung over everybody. For this reason, the submarine captain and the political commissar came to Huang Xuhua, now the chief designer, asking him to boost the team's morale. He pondered it that night. The next day he went into the main meeting room and declared, "I'm going down with you!" The sentence was like water dropping onto a frying pan, and the whole room went into a commotion. There had never been any precedent of a nuclear submarine chief designer personally joining the deep dive test. Furthermore, at the age of 64, he was no longer a young man, and decades of hard work had undermined his health. Everybody was adamantly opposed to the idea, arguing that it was unnecessary for him to take the risk. In sincerity, he replied, "First, we are not diving for 'the ultimate glory' but simply to accumulate test data. Second, our design has offered sufficient safety margins. Third, we have been double-checking for three months. We are confident about the test." His confidence and reminder of the quest for "data" raised the spirits of everyone there. The team was no longer possessed by fear.

Though he did not show it, Huang Xuhua was no less nervous. Success was compulsory now that the project had gone this far. But what if the test failed? He dared not even imagine the consequences. Nevertheless, he was determined to go, just as he had been when he had braved the gunfire in his adolescent years to go to school, and how he had abandoned his childhood dream of studying medicine for a career in shipbuilding. During this time, his wife Li Shiying became his staunchest supporter. They were a like-minded couple as she also worked for the nuclear submarine program. Upon learning his decision, she set aside worry and doubt, and stood by him with firmness, knowing that all her husband needed at the time was unreserved support. Well aware of the danger, she said in a firm tone, "As the chief designer, you are a team leader and must go underwater. Besides, you are responsible for the life of the entire crew." His wife's support strengthened his determination. His confidence and his sense of responsibility as a team leader infected everyone. The team's morale was good, which ensured a smooth, successful test.

Finally, it was the day of the deep dive test — April 29, 1988. The waves were a bit high — over 1 meter — in the South China Sea, but the weather was fine. Everything was in place, and the submarine slowly began diving: 10 meters, 10 meters, 10 meters ... 5 meters, 5 meters, 5 meters ... 1 meter, 1 meter, 1 meter ... In the beginning, the submarine would stop for a while every 10 meters. As it dove deeper, it would stop every 5 meters, and finally, every 1 meter. Water pressure increased with the depth, and the creaking sound of the steel plates under pressure grew increasingly pronounced. Everyone's nerves were on edge as all they could hear was the sound of their own breathing and the creaks of the hull. Huang Xuhua stoically recorded the data with undivided attention until finally the submarine reached the maximum depth — 300 meters. Everything went without a hitch. The vessel remained motionless and intact. Next, the submarine had to float back up to the water surface under the same enormous pressure. The whole crew waited anxiously, their hearts palpitating, as the vessel went up: 280 meters, 200 meters, 150 meters, and 100 meters! The instant the submarine returned to the safe depth, the whole team cheered in excitement, hugging, laughing and crying. Even Huang Xuhua, normally calm and composed, was now beside himself with joy and excitement like everyone else. Everyone knew that the success had not come easy.

Building upon the success of the deep dive test, China completed its underwater missile launch test in the second half of 1988, which meant that China had developed a real underwater nuclear counterattack capability, a deterrent force to solidly defend national security. It was for the purpose of developing China's nuclear submarine program and for national rejuvenation to which Huang Xuhua had dedicated his life. Were there moments of fear or skepticism? Perhaps. But he never flinched at any critical juncture. He steadfastly led the team to blaze a path through all manner of obstacles. A quote from Pavel Korchagin's book *How the Steel Was Tempered* best describes Huang Xuhua's life experience:

"Man's dearest possession is his life. It is given to him but once, and he must live it, so as to never feel regret for wasted years, nor guilty for inaction. In this way, when he is dying, he might be able to say: all my life, all my strength was given to the finest cause in the whole world — the fight for the liberation of mankind."

Chapter Four

Living a Life Not for Fame

"Huang Xuhua! So your life has been remarkable after all!"

Though he has described his achievements as "something remarkable", he has never claimed all the credit. In China, he is hailed as the "father of China's nuclear submarines" — a title he has consistently declined, saying he was just one of the many fighting at the forefront of nuclear submarine research.

He never sought fame or personal prosperity, but remained always optimistic and industrious. These characteristics provide an all-around portrayal of his life.

When he first joined the nuclear submarine program in 1958, he was aware that this top-secret mission would mean hardship and obscurity. He could not tell anyone else about his work, not even his closest relatives. But he accepted the mission without hesitation. For decades, he worked out of the spotlight, content with being an unknown hero in the nuclear submarine program. During this process, the support from his family played a vital role, like the earth's support of a tall tree.

His wife Li Shiying is also a scientist. She has a steady and decisive personality. Their marriage has been a happy one. When Huang went to Beijing and did not return for a long time, she figured out that her husband was involved in some very important mission. She refrained from asking about its details, and nor did she complain. All she did was support her husband's work by real action — taking care of all kinds of housework and bringing up their children on her own. Later, she moved from Shanghai to Beijing, taking along the children, and from there to the island where Huang Xuhua worked. During those years on the island, Li Shiying would have to carry hundreds of kilograms of coal briquettes home every winter, assisted by her children. Even during those difficult days when she managed the household by herself, she retained her sense of humor. Whenever Huang Xuhua would return home on vacation, she would greet him jokingly, "So the guest has come back!" In return, he would readily accept the greeting and hail himself as a "guest", too. He would not stay very long, but would come and go in a hurry, normally staying at home for less than one day before he'd go back to the research institute again. Looking back on these experiences, he feels deeply indebted to his family.

Among those who made sacrifices were also his elderly parents. Due to the secrecy of the project, he was not allowed to tell them what he was doing. It was not until 1987 that his mother got to know that he had been working for China's nuclear submarine program. Subsequently, she called a special family meeting to clear up any misunderstandings, telling them to be proud of his work.

China's nuclear submarine program would not have developed so fast without the dedication of numerous scientists like Huang Xuhua and the support from their families. After the success, Huang Xuhua would speak candidly at every interview, "I love my wife. I love my mother. I love my daughters. I love them all." An old man who had been born in the 1920s, he speaks of love with such perfect candour and warmth because he owes a lot to his family and because of his deep feelings towards them. His family are dear to him, but still dearer is the nation. He never regrets the choice he made in his youth.

Building a nuclear submarine was by no means a lucrative job as some outsiders might think. What faced Huang Xuhua and his colleagues were not just technical challenges, but material shortages and the hard living conditions. Yet he overcame all these difficulties thanks to his endurance, perseverance, and optimism.

As the nuclear submarine project made progress, the team needed to move to different sites. For a rather long period of time, Huang Xuhua and his colleagues stayed on a desolate island — Huludao, an extremely cold place. When Huang Xuhua, a native of southern China, first stepped onto the island, the high winds dealt him a head-on blow. They were freezing and strong, howling from all sides and threatening to scrape the ground open, and the whole world turned dusty. An adult would lose his balance amid such fierce gales, and would not be able to hold his footing unless he clung to a tree trunk. Hence the team jokingly called such strong gales a "tree-embracing wind". In such an inhospitable environment, surely the living conditions would be made a bit more comfortable for them. Actually, no. On this island, meat and fish were often absent from their diet, and these young scientists, whose average age was under 30, often felt underfed.

"What's for breakfast today?"

"Cabbage stewed with cabbage!"

"What's for lunch then?"

"Potatoes stewed with cabbage!"

"Then supper?"

"Potatoes stewed with potatoes!"

…

Conversations like this took place almost every day. In those days, the most exciting thing for Huang

Xuhua and his colleagues was eating "red cubes". Whenever the "red cubes" were served, the whole day would be full of laughter.

"What are we eating today?"

"Red cubes!"

"Oh, red cubes! Great! Then I think I'll have two bowlfuls of sorghum rice today!"

"If my memory serves, your stomach is big enough for only one bowl. Don't eat more than you can chew. Spare the second bowl and leave it to me. Let me do the job for you."

"No! With red cubes, I can handle any number of bowls of rice offered."

...

So what was the so-called red cube which they loved

so much? Believe it or not, it was fermented bean curd. For Huang Xuhua and his colleagues, whose diets rarely went beyond potatoes and Chinese cabbage, a few pieces of fermented bean curd with sorghum rice was a fabulous meal. When he recalls those difficult years today, he is impressed less by their hardships than by their joys. To remain optimistic and find joy in the face of simple material conditions is in the blood of Chinese culture.

Perhaps it was owing to Huang Xuhua's steadfast enthusiasm in the face of hardships that great accomplishments were made in the nuclear submarine program. But behind the enthusiasm was his indifference to fame and gain, and an endless supply of endurance, perseverance, optimism, resourcefulness, patriotism and dedication.

Today, Huang Xuhua is still fulfilling his pledge. In his 90's, this amiable old man looks just like a common grandpa who lives next door. Though he is no longer directly engaged in nuclear submarine research and development, he has made it a rule to come to his office at 8:30 every morning. He sorts through information, data, records and documents that have accumulated over the decades of research work, with an eye to building up an archive for future reference. Sometimes he offers guidance and encouragement to the younger generations of nuclear submarine scientists. He has never stopped working, even during the latter half of his life. To go on making some contributions in his remaining years — this is Huang Xuhua's real wish.

The lyrics composed by lyricist Yan Su in 2014 dedicated to Huang Xuhua give the best description of his life experience:

What is it like to dedicate oneself to the nation?

Let me ask the vast ocean.

Black hair has turned gray,

But keeping fighting remains his aspiration.

His is a life of grandeur and immense love,

Voiced in a tune speechless, but laden with passion.

出版策划：王君校　韩　晖
统筹协调：付　眉　韩　颖　彭　博
责任编辑：杨　晗
英文编辑：卢　敏
插画绘制：胡美慧
封面设计：智玖拾（成都）文化传媒有限公司
印刷监制：汪　洋

图书在版编目（CIP）数据

黄旭华：汉英对照 / 江雪编著；吴洲翻译. -- 北京：华语教学出版社，2021.4
（中国时代先锋人物）
ISBN 978-7-5138-2103-2

Ⅰ．①黄… Ⅱ．①江… ②吴…Ⅲ．①黄旭华－生平事迹 Ⅳ．① D263

中国版本图书馆 CIP 数据核字（2021）第 051944 号

中国时代先锋人物：黄旭华

江雪　编著
吴洲　翻译

*

© 华语教学出版社有限责任公司
华语教学出版社有限责任公司出版
（中国北京百万庄大街 24 号　邮政编码 100037）
电话：(86)10-68320585, 68997826
传真：(86)10-68997826, 68326333
网址：www.sinolingua.com.cn
电子信箱：hyjx@sinolingua.com.cn
北京虎彩文化传播有限公司印刷
2021 年（32 开）第 1 版
2024 年第 1 版第 4 次印刷
ISBN 978-7-5138-2103-2
003990